A Tale of Crofting

Alex McGlashen

Alex McGlashen reserves the right to
be identified as the author of this work
All rights reserved. No part of this publication may be
reproduced, stored in a retrieval system, or transmitted in any form or by
means, electronic, mechanical, photocopying, recording or otherwise,
without the prior permission of the publishers.

This first edition published May 2025

ISBN 978-1-7384141-7-8

Cover design and artwork
by Tricky Imp
Illustrations by Tricky Imp and Alex McGlashen

More Information at:
www.trickyimp.com

Published by Tricky Imp

Printed in the United Kingdom by 4edge

FOREWORD

Though there are still crofters in Scotland, it is safe to say that both the process and the lifestyle of the old crofting ways have gone, with the exception of a handful of historically based projects and stoic traditionalists. The machinery, tools and the way of life to a certain degree have been relegated to museums and private collections and in a few more generations all that was once part of a way of life will be but a distant memory. There are, however, a few people still alive at the time of writing this book, who were either brought up as children within the community of crofting or who actively participated in that lifestyle when they were young. These people are generally in their eighties or older and for this reason, I undertook to try and glean some first-hand information about their early experiences living on the land. There are also a few people who are not so old, who still remember their grandparents living the crofting lifestyle and staying in steadings of the traditional type.

Those old steadings or homesteads, built of stone with clay mortar and thatched or earth roofs are very few these days, but certainly, in parts of the Highlands and Far North, many of these structures can be seen, long since abandoned or in some cases renovated for modern living. They are very stylised and easy to identify as for the most part they were almost identical in their plan and elevation. Many were remote and had no more than tracks to reach them with little or no amenities, which is why few of them have been preserved. These tiny steadings were a slight improvement on an earlier stone building known as a 'Blackhouse' and retained many similar features of this type of building.

There is not the space in this small volume to delve deeply into either the architecture or the evolution of the crofter's world but I will certainly endeavour to explain what I can. We will explore their steadings, their working day, diet and clothing along with the problems associated with the daily life of the crofter. The period covered will mainly be concerned with a date from the 1890s up to the 1950s as this is the period that covers the memories of the people I have spoken with. That said, I will also explore incidents in earlier times that formed what the crofters became and what broke their world apart.

This is not a history of the crofter. Neither is it a definitive treatise on crofting, far from it. Nor will I cover the dark period of the Clearances with any detail as there are more specific accounts of that by many authors. This is a collection of accounts from a two-year period of research and speaking with the people still living, who remember either the stories of their families or memories of their own time within the crofting community. This book could be described as an anecdotal account covering the whole of the crofting period from the mid-1780s, to the 1960s. It is a general, 'from the horse's mouth' reminiscence by people who recall those days with some historical context thrown in for good measure. Many of them say that though they wouldn't want to return to those times, they remember their experiences with fondness. It was a quieter, steadier time yet full of the harshness and uncertainty that came from the hard task of surviving in such a harsh climate. It was hard work too and yet so often I see long and healthy lives among these people.

I am greatly indebted to many people I have spoken to over the two years I have been collecting these stories. I have talked with so many people and in some cases, I have no names to credit them with their tales. A few do not even wish their names to appear. For those that I do know, their names appear in the rear of the book but to everyone who dedicated much of their time to relating their stories to me, I thank them for helping me preserve their stories and heritage in print.

A Tale of Crofting

A Short History of Crofting

If you look at most histories of crofting, you will probably read that crofting was a product of the Clearances but I do not fully agree with this. I accept that the word crofting didn't come into general use until the 1886 Crofting Act but it was used prior to this. If we consider that crofting is small-scale tenanted farming, then this was being practised long before the clearances. I rather think that crofting was the end product of an evolution rather than an overnight policy.

The Croft was historically similar to the Cottage of England (originally the name cottage referred to the land, not the house) where a plot of land was farmed by a tenant of the landowner or more accurately, the Bailiff of the landowner.

The land area could vary a great deal in England as in Scotland but generally, land was gauged by its yield rather than its square yardage. The measurement of this was set in yardlands, sometimes called virgate. As it was assessed by yield, this could range between fifteen and forty acres but on the whole was about thirty acres. In Scotland, areas that came under Danelaw would be more likely to measure in the ancient system of 'oxgangs'. (This measurement is also considered to be older and likely to be a Pict measurement which the Vikings took as their own.) Two oxgangs would be about the same as a virgate but rarely would this be an accurate measurement. In England, there were further measurements including such rustic names as 'nooks' and 'farundels'. An oxgang represented an amount of land that could be worked by an ox pulling a plough, so our thirty acres would be partitioned as 'two oxgangs' as in a ploughing season, a single ox could cover around fifteen acres.

It is interesting to note that an acre was considered the amount of land that a single man could till with one ox in one day.

The use of the oxgang measurement in Scotland is explained by the word 'Davoch' which is cognate by the Gaelic 'dabhach', the word 'dahb' meaning ox.

In Scotland where the fertility of the land was less important, the land was more usually gauged by how much grazing the land would allow. Research shows that in the East, the measurement was different to the West. This is probably due to the different languages on the two coasts more than the use of the land. For instance: eight oxgangs translated to a 'ploughgate' and there were four ploughgates to a Davoch. In the West we have 'pennylands' and 'ouncelands', there being twenty pennylands to the dabhach or davoch. You can see that it is easy with set measurements to see land in area, but the crofter of the day would see it more as a measure of content. Rather than saying it is so many acres, he would measure it in barrels of potatoes or cartloads of turnips. In the earliest times, these measurements must have been large indeed as a davoch could have been over one hundred acres in certain parts of the Highlands.

In Scotland, the system was very similar with the 'tacksman' fulfilling a similar role to the bailiff and it was they who partitioned and rented out the land for the owner. The earliest systems in both England and Scotland were a product of the feudal system and though the Highlands had a different character to it, the Clan system was certainly a feudal system in its day-to-day operation. At the height of the Clan system, the landowner or the chief parcelled out his land and gave the better and more productive land to his closest family and sometimes to valued retainers. In earlier times, there would be fewer people and therefore more land but as the population grew and the Clan Chiefs required more men to protect their lands from other clans, the land available became more overcrowded. There was plenty of land of course but little that was fertile or useful for farming. The poor ground was improved a little but yields would be small on such land. Summer pastures on higher ground were used but in the winter this land would be untenable. The grazing land was communal and this led to bad management of that land which caused its own problems.

Cattle theft became a real problem so extra retainers were needed to protect land and cattle and these retainers needed their own land. A vicious circle as you can see. This set clan against clan, and sometimes brother against brother and father against son. Inside the clan land, the run-rig system developed though the system was probably an evolution from the medieval period. The land was divided into townships which had the more fertile land called 'in-bye' and then rough pasture land around it. The system varied from place to place but it was similar to communal farming. The land was divided into strips, and each tenant farmed a strip. Each strip would have a crop and each year the crop in each strip changed. In some townships, lots were drawn to ensure a single tenant didn't always get the most fertile land. The system eventually died out as fixed tenancy became more usual and so the crofting system arrived.

The crofting system is said to have started in Argyll as early as the 1770s but there is evidence to show that this was a steady movement from the run-rig system as stated previously. The early crofts were of a size that could provide a comfortable living for a family. Crofts of around thirty acres on good land could easily sustain a reasonable size of family. This would not be the case in the later period. The crofting system of tenure was generally adopted by all Highland landowners as a part of their so-called improvement programmes. It enabled them to bring the crofting population directly under their control and move them at will. It soon became the habit of the landowner to provide smaller crofts to ensure that the tenant could not survive without gaining other employment, usually from the landowner for other duties. It is usually considered that the crofter could find himself working at the mercy of the landowner for up to 200 days a year. This employment could be just about anything, from maintenance, wall and ditch building, fishing and work within the kelp trade. This put much pressure on the crofter and made him a virtual slave to the landowner.

In law, a crofter was an agricultural tenant in occupation of a piece of land owned by a landlord on a year-to-year basis. Therefore, the landlord was entitled to terminate the crofter's tenancy at the end of any year and recover possession of the land, together with any buildings and other permanent improvements that might have been completed on the croft and its buildings.

The tenant had no claim against the landlord whatsoever and received no compensation for improvements. This is why tenants did not build good homes for their families and why to the eyes of the visiting public, their houses looked nothing more than hovels. Their livelihood and the roof over their head were temporary.

The Crofters Act of 1886 was supposed to change that but to start with it made little impact. It purported to provide security of tenure for all those who were tenants of crofts at that time, irrespective of how small the croft was. Of course, the condition of tenancy was that the crofter should pay his rent regularly nor allow the croft and buildings to deteriorate. He was not allowed to subdivide his croft without the landlord's consent, and not become bankrupt. The truth is, the landlords didn't like the act and for the most part ignored it. After all, who was going to argue with wealthy landowners who lived in Edinburgh or London and were probably magistrates or members of Parliament?

The Croft Byre

Eventually, the Land Court was established to determine fair rent on application by either the landlord or the crofter. Once the Land Court fixed the croft rent, it would stand for seven years unless altered by mutual agreement. Rent–racking, which saw some rents double in the year following, still continued here and there until the issues were brought before the Land Court.

The right of the crofter to claim compensation from his landlord for the permanent improvements was also part of the act. Improvements which were considered suitable to the croft, or paid for by the crofter would gain compensation should he renounce the croft or be removed from it.

Probably the most important part of the Act was the right of the crofter to bequeath his croft to a member of his family as well as the right to cut peats and gather seaweed. This more than anything else gave the crofter security and almost immediately the steading and croft dwellings improved and became a more permanent house giving the crofter a sense of belonging and pride he or she had not experienced previously.

Sadly, an important feature of the crofting system was omitted from the act. The common grazing of a highland township is critical, yet the 1886 Crofters Act made no provision for its administration. The run-rig system had a township official called a constable who was elected by the crofters to handle issues and report them to the landlord or his factor. Under the Act, there was no administration of the common grazing but in a subsequent revision in 1891, this was rectified. The first Crofters Commission admitted that their greatest source of trouble had been the management of the common grazing.

In my opinion, the Act failed to secure the livelihood of the crofter as most of the damage was already done due to the vast number of people cleared from the land by the time the Act entered the statute. Not only that, the Act only provided protection for those who held crofts. The landless cotter remained landless and continued as a slave to anyone who would employ him.

It was a step in the right direction but even at the time of the Act, there were still crofters being cleared for vast new sheep farms.

The government had been expected to take steps to break up these large farms and deer parks and so the cottars and their families were bitterly disappointed when they realised that there was no provision in the act for new landholdings. Their help by Parliamentary action was now gone and past experience had taught them they would get no sympathy or justice from the greedy landlords. The magistrates and the church had helped landlords to clear the land and so many considered there was no option for them.

Then came the depression of the 1880s and the cottars were forced to live in barns and rough shelters without hope of ever being relieved except by ignoring the laws and raiding the former crofter townships now flooded with sheep, and staking out crofts for themselves.

Part of a Crofting township

This would bring trouble and the famous Park Deer raid which found much publicity in 1887 was the start of it, soon followed by many land raids in the Park

Deer Forest in 1891. Many cottars would find themselves in prison and some were transported, others left the land to an unknown future.

It wasn't until the Act of 1911 that this problem was addressed and repatriation was begun, but the Great War of 1914 saw many of them killed in France before they had the chance to taste anything like freedom. Those who did return took advantage of the new Act.

There were still many hard times to come for the crofters and yet another war saw many not return to their crofts. The Highlander has always answered the call to arms when needed which is ironic given the way he has been treated by Britain. But he has always volunteered in great numbers.

A major advancement for the crofter came in 1976 with the right for many crofters to purchase the croft they lived and worked upon, but that was fine if you could afford to do so. The crofts have become smaller over the years and few crofters could make a living from their land alone. Today, there are still many crofts and many crofters too but the problems remain, that in this harsh land with small plots and a short season, it is difficult, very difficult, to make a living from a croft.

The Crofter

There are many accounts throughout history which include descriptions of the Highland crofter and few are even slightly complimentary. I think this has a great deal to do with the fact that in history, the crofter usually spoke the Gaelic language and few knew English or Scot. This more than anything sets them apart. Added to the fact that they had few possessions, lived in houses with turf roofs, dressed differently and had a complexion that went with living on the land, they must have seemed like aliens to town people even before they opened their mouths to speak.

An Italian tourist travelling the Highlands in the 1850s remarked that the crofters were living in filth and shared their hovels with vermin. Several other commentators through history have expanded on this image and though we cannot know the exact circumstances under which these views were first gathered, we have to remember that a passing tourist who had the means to travel Europe at that time would have the wealth and background that would make his opinion of a people he didn't understand a pointless observation. Yes, they were poor, and yes, wherever there are ears of grain and thatched roofs, rats are bound to proliferate. This was still the case even in the 1950s as we will see later, but to take a great deal from these comments would leave us in error about these oppressed people. They were also described by wealthy landowners and churchmen as idle and slovenly. This is probably more to do with the misunderstanding of their way of life than any detailed observation. Living in the far north, then as it is today, the growing season is very short and in the winter half of the year, there is little light in the late afternoon. This lifestyle ensures that when they were busy in the times of harvesting, they were *very* busy, but the short season meant that there was little to do late in the year and few daylight hours in which to do it. Is this why they seemed lazy to people without an understanding of their way of life?

So, what is a crofter? In ancient times, cattle would be grazed on higher pastures in the summer and brought down to lower and more fertile land in the winter. This meant that the life of a herder was tough and his shelter was transient with the idea of permanent dwellings being alien. Even at the time of the clans, this lifestyle continued and the drovers would make temporary shelters for the season. Some made tiny shelters from branches, earth and stone, others made small stone structures covered with bracken and turf. I have even seen an old woodcut showing a similar construction to North American-style tee-pee dwellings. These were expanded upon over time into better-constructed stone buildings bonded with clay mortar to keep the weather out and a timber-framed roof covered with turf and or thatch. As windows allowed the weather in, they were omitted and a very basic door was fitted made from wood or in some cases fabric. In realistic terms, these people are drovers and not crofters but this is the background to one of the lifestyles of these people.

These drovers lived with the animals they protected and would move them around the Highlands from one grazing area to another. Being the Highlands, this meant crossing water quite often and this was a big problem. Two European travellers in Scotland in 1786 witnessed drovers about their business and stated,

"when they drive these cattle through the hills. which are as one must see divided by a great many lochs, they never let even the more valuable cattle go by boat, but make them swim across all the waters they come to on their drove roads; and they have told me they very seldom lose one. These cows are almost always black, and often well-formed and good-looking."

An engraving from a French magazine, 1833 Entitled Scotch Cattle Drovers.

Another mention of a crossing of water comes from 1730 in, 'Northern Rural Life in the 18th Century'.

"The cows were about fifty in number, and took the water like spaniels; and when they were in their drivers made a hideous cry to urge them forwards; this they did they told me to keep the foremost of them from turning about, for in that case the rest would do the like, and they could be in danger, especially the weakest of them, to be driven away and drowned by the torrent. I thought it a very odd sight to see so many noses and eyes just above the

water, and nothing of them more to be seen, for they had no horns and upon the land they appeared like so many Lincolnshire calves."

An engraving showing drovers taking cattle to the Ballachulish Ferry seen on the right of the image.

It was a hard life for both the cattle and the drovers as stated in Alastair Mitchell's excellent book, The Immeasurable Wilds, Quoting from James Mitchell's work he writes,

"Cattle reared in Caithness and the Orkneys were driven across the mountains by land, and when they reached the more favoured pastures of the south, some 300 or 400 miles away, they were little more than skin and bone. The drovers called them

the 'Caithness Runts': very ungainly-looking animals."

Even in the golden age of the clans, this lifestyle persisted and the clan chief would carve up his land to be rented out by what were called tacksmen, usually the closest relatives to the clan chief. We have touched on this earlier but the tacksman sub-divided these plots of land further to sub-tenants who farmed that plot and paid rent for it. Eventually, several of these tenants would build more permanent dwellings in a loose collection scattered over an area, and they became known as townships.

As these tenants had sons, the sons themselves in time would need their own land so the father would in turn carve up his land. This ongoing process led to a major problem as the land for each family became smaller over each generation. Eventually, the land became so small that a living could not be made from it.

This system also meant that more dwellings used land too, and so the farmers became poorer as the usable land shrank. The dwellings did improve however and eventually the traditional 'Blackhouse' evolved. There is much conjecture of why they are called Blackhouses but I tend to agree with the Isle of Lewis explanation.

A central open hearth.

It is said that the reason for the name isn't due to the soot from the open-hearth fires, or even due to the darkness from lack of windows, but because when the animals became separated into their own barns rather than sharing the living space with the family, the distinction was made between the two dwellings. The newer building was for the people to live in, probably being called a Whitehouse to make the distinction between the two. This is also logical due to the later use of limewash on clay-mortared walls. Limewash holds back the growth of moss in damper climates and seeing as moss damages the mortar, the newer dwellings would probably be painted white. Either way, the Blackhouse developed eventually into the Butt and Ben and later the longhouse which can both still be seen over many parts of Caithness and the rest of the Highlands.

On the subject of the dwellings, particularly in the areas where trees rarely grow, the roof timbers would be highly prised and could be old timbers from other buildings or even from shipwrecks. This meant that roof timbers were hardly ever left behind when a family moved and the timbers were as important as other furniture. Some had probably been owned for generations, which is probably why the landowner's factor would burn down the houses during the clearances. This disgraceful practice not only left people without a place to live, it robbed them of their heritage and the heirlooms of their roof timbers. We know that some people were seriously burned trying to remove beams from their burning houses.

It is true that thousands of people were removed from their crofts and the number could be much higher than estimates have previously stated. Many of these people left the land for good to seek new lives in other countries, though some didn't survive the perilous journey. Those that did, on occasion made better lives for themselves but we know this was not always true. Some of course stayed, and it seems this depended on location and a variable set of circumstances. Those that tried to ride out the storm would either survive or not, and could even succumb to later purges of the croft land to reuse the glens for sheep farming. In later years the pattern of clearances altered and when some landowners tried to raise troops for the wars with France, they found few men capable of going to war and were told by some of the crofters to give the muskets to the sheep that now occupied the hills.

In some instances, the crofters fought back but these so-called 'crofter's wars' were never going to stop the march of commercial progress. As I have mentioned previously, as a general rule, the crofter knew the language of his ancestors, Gaelic. This language was a Western language inherited from the Irish tongue, Historically, Scotland had always been a land of more than one language and some had come and gone leaving remnants of them behind. The original language of the Picts was an old Celtic tongue that had spread throughout the British Isles. It lived at the side of another Celtic language that had spread on the western coast of Europe and made its way from Brittany all the way north to the Hebrides and Ireland. These two early languages became an east and west divide with trade and some travel leaving some to which both languages could be understood. We know these languages today as P and Q Celtic. Q Celtic would morph into the Brittonic language of Wales and Cornish whilst P Celtic would eventually become English. To add to this, a sort of halfway-house language became the common tongue of the lowland areas and became the more traditional Scots language. Then came the Romans and though they had little influence on the languages in the north, their legacy continued in the text and teachings of the Catholic Church, Latin. The Presbyterian religion did not use as much Latin but it did remain in the background. Of course, the Vikings had a great impact on both sociological and linguistic aspects of Scotland but there are few words from the Vikings left in the language on the mainland. Then came the most influential language, the language of numbers and accounting. The language of money. It was this language that changed the world for the crofter more than anything else. Even before Culloden, the clan chiefs were marrying daughters of lowland merchants to bring in substantial dowries. After Culloden, this became more pronounced as the heads of the clans that had assisted the government against the Jacobite cause received lands from deposed landowners. These chiefs married into a society they had previously had little connection to but these wives from wealthy merchants and influential families didn't want to live in the harsh environment of the Highlands. They wanted townhouses in Edinburgh or even London. This lifestyle cost money and the language of money became the language of the clan chief. Most became absentee landlords and sold out the people they had once protected. The same people who had supported them. Crofters were removed to make more profits from sheep farming and rented out to lowland businessmen.

It is considered that the Duke of Sutherland had a yearly income of £350,000 and was one of the wealthiest men in the world, but it didn't stop him and his wife from trying to make more by ridding the Highlands of its people. Their factors held one particular meeting in the village of Golspie and told the tenants to be there. The tenants came but as the speech to tell them they were being moved from their crofts was in English, they returned home not understanding why they had been told to attend. Not until a month later the factor came to turn them out and burn their homes. In their small communities where Gaelic was the only language that was ever needed, they had not seen that the world had changed and the language of commerce and now Scotland, was solely English, and you cannot fight what you do not understand.

We could call it 'ethnic cleansing', but that is not what it was. The crofters were not moved just because they were Gaels. Not even because they were different.

They were moved on because they were not profitable because, in the past, rent was sometimes paid in kind by working for the landowner. That wasn't good enough for the modern Scottish landowner. Cash was what he craved, and as much as he could get. It was simply business.

Over the years, the political landscape changed and newspapers developed in the area and brought the plight of the crofter to the attention of a wider audience. This turned public opinion and even in England people looked at the plight of the crofter and brought about change. The change was slow and gradual but this didn't stop the landowners from breaking these new laws. As stated earlier, the Crofters Acts did improve the stability of the crofter's life. This did not, always prevent rent-racking however, which saw some crofters see a fifty per cent rise in rents from one year to the next. In Clyth in Caithness, the crofters stopped paying their rent and met with the landowner who was of course unsympathetic. He pointed out that they were breaking the law and would evict them if they didn't pay. That essentially was the end of their protest. There were laws on both sides, but generally as is still the case today, they favoured the wealthy, not the poor.

There were also boom times and I have certainly heard stories of how well the crofters did during the many wars that Britain found itself involved in. But alas, the crofter's economic system was fatally flawed and in the, many turned their back on that way of life to join the modern world and all the problems that it brings.

Today, there are still many registered crofts and many crofters but few of them can make a living from the system and usually turn to other means to supplement their income.

A Traditional Butt and Ben house with byre added. This is a typical shape and size of crofting house in the middle of the nineteenth century. Later, the byre would become part of the main building and another section would be added at the opposite end. This would be the stables where there would be enough space for two Highland ponies to live.

The Crofter's Dwelling

Mention has already been made of the style and structure of the crofter's dwelling but I wish to explain the interior to the reader.

To a degree, after the period where the animals shared the same building, the steading would be furnished in a similar fashion to other houses with basic cupboards and sideboards for keeping the items the crofter owned. Differences appeared in the manner of their beds and their fireplaces. They had an open-hearth fire to cook and heat water upon as well as to warm the room. In the early period, there was no chimney and the smoke was supposed to exit through vents in the eaves. During the 1800s, chimneys became more popular but with the unwelcome drawback of an increase of rats in the thatch due to a less toxic environment for the wee beasts. Thatch has always made an ideal home for rats and it has been a burden carried by the crofter throughout the period. Even the most dedicated cat can only catch so many rats and sometimes a dog was kept and trained for this purpose. The floor beneath was usually of earth but some steadings did have stone flag floors which enabled the house to be swept reasonably clean.

In most cases, the walls were painted with limewash and later in the period, window shutters were replaced with glass and internal covers for the more inclement times of the season.

Lighting was by cruise or cruisie lamps, or rush lamps which in Caithness were sometimes known as 'blacknebs'. These gave as much light as a candle but were cheaper than tallow candles using straw or reed for their wick. Oil was usually made by fishermen from the throwaway parts of their catch. It is likely that the smell from these lamps would mix with the smoke from the peat fires to give a very distinctive aroma in the croft.

The beds were usually 'box beds' or in blackhouses a hole in the void of the very thick walls. Box beds were around in Tudor times and were essentially a large wooden cupboard, sometimes freestanding which would keep the family from the cold of a dafty house. A mattress filled with straw or sometimes horse hair provided comfort and after trying one of these beds I can affirm that they can be made very cosy. If there were two rooms in the dwelling, one room would be for the beds, the other for cooking and living in. This would be the kitchen and dining area, usually with a simple wooden table in the centre. The croft houses known as 'Butt and Ben' were of this type with just two rooms, sometimes with a small closet between them. By this period the animals would usually be kept in a separate building or in an extension to the steading called a byre.

Running water would rarely be a feature and I know of several steadings still being worked in the 1950s and 1960s that never had running water, cold or otherwise. The water was usually drawn from a well and carried to the home with pails or buckets. Electricity too was something that few croft houses ever received. It is easy to quickly pass over this reality but I have tried this way of life and the need to fetch every pint of water from a well soon alters the habits of the household. I can assure you that this makes even the most simple of tasks a major chore. Of course, any hot water required had to be boiled on the fire in kettles or larger cast iron pans.

Washing and bathing were done by the fire too and so privacy was a preference not easily attained. I was born into a very austere household not many years after the Second World War and though many people would consider this time modern, in some ways, particularly for the poorer families, it was little changed from the 1850s. Therefore, I have my own stories to tell of my formative years and one such story concerns the tin bath. In earlier times, the household bath could be quite small, similar to something known as a hip bath. Water would be heated on the fire and poured straight from the large kettle into the bath or wooden tub. In my childhood, we had a larger tin bath that could usually be seen hanging on a nail by the outside toilet door. This was brought in and placed by the fire where the family would take turns bathing, from the master of the house, down to the youngest child. If it was a large family, the water would be less than in its prime and it is likely that the term, 'don't throw the baby out with the bathwater' comes from, the water being too dirty to tell if the baby was still in there. I was very lucky indeed as I was an only child.

Clothes were washed in wooden or iron tubs too and the grime was removed by washboards and scrubbing brushes. This may on occasions have been done with leftover bath water if it wasn't too tainted. The general clothing was agitated by means of a dolly, sometimes called a posser, poncher, or ponch. These were generally made of wood but later ones made of copper were sometimes seen. Of course, this was done by hand. Nothing was automated. Once the clothes were washed and rinsed, they would be wrung out by hand and if the home had a mangle, the clothing would be forced between the tight wooden rollers to extract as much water as possible.

Wooden dolly in a galvanised metal tub.

I have another story of my own on this matter. I have two embarrassing photographs of myself. One I will not admit to here. The other is of myself at the age of three or four years, stripped down to my underpants and standing by the 'ponch-tub' covered in suds. This it seems was children's entertainment in those long-ago days when the height of fun was to help on wash day though I suspect it was more about wetting everywhere through rather than a concerted effort to help with chores.

I also recall my gran having to remove all the buttons of my grandad's shirts lest the mangle smashed the delicate shell buttons. When removed, the shirts were washed, rinsed and sent through the mangle then hung on the washing line. When dry, she would press them with a hot iron, (heated on the fire) and then the buttons were sewn back on. Consider this the next time you throw your modern clothing in the automatic washing machine.

The need for all this utilitarian equipment would also dictate the look of the interior of the house too. Very little that could be seen in the crofter's home was ornamental and everything on a shelf or hung on the nail in the wall would have some purpose or other. The more I have learned about the life of these people, the greater is my admiration for the women folk who seemed to have an endless list of chores and I simply can't imagine how they got time for everything. With all this work, my own gran always had a pure white doorstep and all the fire blackwork on the range gleamed as if it was new, as did all brass candlesticks and lamps.

She had a pride in her home that went far above that which we would understand today.

The mangle. The wooden rollers were tightened by the wheel on the top.

Everything in the home, including tools and equipment had to be maintained by the family and this included clothing and footwear. My grandad had an odd-shaped tool called a hobbin foot or cobbler's last, which was used to repair boots and shoes. It was a large cast iron affair and at least one saying was developed from it. My grandmother would explain her wish for food away by saying,

'I'm so hungry, I could eat a hobbin foot.'

There was also a practice to which I have seen little information about but I know it was something that was done latterly, if not in the earlier times. Where a steading had a thatch over turf, or even just turf roofs, the turf itself would constantly shed debris particularly when the weather was windy and the turf was old.

A hobbin foot or cobbler's last

To try to prevent this and keep the home a little cleaner, cheap paper such as wallpaper would be nailed over the roof beams to hide the underside of the turf. This was then painted with limewash or thin white paint which helped with the reflectivity of any light entering the house. Of course, when the paper dried out, it would become crinkly and would look a little rough and ready, but it kept debris out of your porridge.

On the subject of porridge, many crofters had a particular drawer in their house called, the porridge drawer. This could be in a sideboard or even under one of the box beds. A large pot of porridge was readied on the fire and once it was cooked, it was poured into the porridge draw and left to set. If this was in the box bed it was usual to do this at night so as to provide under-bed heating in winter. Once the porridge was set, it could be cut or broken up and taken as a snack or out to the field when off to work. I have been told by a few people that as children, they would come home from school and raid the porridge drawer as soon as they arrived. The porridge drawer that was sited under the box bed was also used as a makeshift crib and I have heard many say that they slept in such as a child.

Oats are a fabulous crop and have been grown as a staple of the Highlands for hundreds of years. Though the variety of oats grown has changed, they remain basically the same crop. Black Oats, sometimes called Japanese Oats, were the original crop grown by crofters in most areas, and over the years the methods of growing this crop are little changed. Its importance to the livelihood of the crofter and economy of the area cannot be overstated, Meal as it was generally known, was exported south by ship and eventually by rail through the period. Black Oats are now grown mainly as a soil improver but the type is hardy and prolific with the possibility of becoming a weed in other crops if not managed well.

Oats are also the main ingredient of Scottish oatcakes which are still made and eaten all around the country. Oats can be grown on ground that is unsuitable for other crops and can withstand a variety of unpleasant environments yet still give a reasonable yield, making it ideal for the Scottish climate and the rougher land of the crofter. Oats have also been important for their ruggedness and were partly responsible for lessening the effect of the two great potato famines in Scotland. In Ireland, the blight of the potato caused a great deal of problems to the poorer people and many starved as the potato crop rotted, yet in Scotland the dependency on the potato hadn't been so great due to the continuing meal trade and so the famine wasn't quite as severe in some areas.

The crofter would also make oatcakes which were easy and quick to produce with the basic ingredient being oats, mixed with water, salt, butter or lard. It was kneaded and rolled into a large flat pancake. This was then dropped onto a 'girdle' or skillet, sometimes just a frying pan and cooked until hard on both sides. There was also a purpose-built girdle for toasting oatcakes which would be a treasured item but mainly they were made in whatever the family possessed.
Porridge was made similar to a gruel and everyone had their own way of making it. Sometimes, whey or milk was added but the basic ingredients were oats in water seasoned with salt. These days, porridge tends to be eaten as a sweet dish but through most of the crofting communities, it was considered a more savoury meal and could on occasions include onions and other scraps of vegetables.

Oats were a very important crop to the crofter. The old 'black oats', sometimes called Japanese oats are grown as a soil improver in more modern times.

Peat Cutting

The peat was very important to the crofter for many reasons. It kept you warm as it burned on the fire, it dried your clothes, heated your water and cooked and smoked your food. It had many other uses too but these are the primary reasons for cutting peat.

It is a heavy, messy job if the land is wet but fortunately, the task can be completed quickly if two are employed to do it. A good amount can be cut in a single day and the experienced crofter and his family could cut enough in a week to last him the whole year.

Every seam of peat is different to the next and peat on Shetland is different to Orkney, and peat on the Islands is different to that in Caithness. It is the nature and the long history of peat that makes these differences. Peat also has a sort of grain and working with that grain can make the task easier.

Wherever it is cut, the method and the tools differ little although there are two distinct methods of cutting it. It can be cut from above, which is sometimes called damming or it can be cut on the horizontal which is broaching. This depends on the peat as well as the cutter.

The Tusker looks like a weapon of war.

There are three main tools for cutting peat. The first one is for removing the heather layer which is probably the hardest job. The tool is called a flaughter and the larger ones are designed so that the hips can be brought into play to thrust the blade through the fibrous roots. Then the cuts are made to allow cutting into the top layer. This is done with a rutter which is a large blade with a handle. A spade can do a similar job too. The actual peats are cut with a tool that looks like a medieval weapon of war. It is called a Tairsgeir pronounced Tusker. There are as many different designs of this tool as there are peat banks but they are all similar in style if not size. As a bit of fun, I used to tell tourists that Scottish peats were cut larger than Irish peats because Scotsmen are stronger, but the truth is that the quality of peat, its grain and its water content can dictate how large it is cut and this only comes from experience.

A very tidy peat stack.

The best peat comes low in the seam and as the bank creeps forward over consecutive years of cutting, the top layer should be replaced to keep the area tidy and allow the heather to regrow on the removed peat. The best time to cut depending on the climate is late spring or early summer. Orkney peat banks can flood easily so dryer times are best.

As the peat is cut, it is lifted onto the bank, then several peats are arranged and left where they are to dry out. This process can be quick depending on the peat but may take a fortnight to three weeks. Once it is ready for moving, the peats are loaded onto a cart and taken to the croft where they are built into a wall, or a mound where they will remain until required.

Should we still cut Peats? It is widely known now that peat holds a great deal of carbon and so the peat beds need to be protected by keeping the water level high sealing the carbon in. But the truth is, our planet is vastly overpopulated and blaming the cutting of peat on the greater failures of man cures nothing. We should manage our resources and population numbers better. I think the greater damage done on peat banks is when the cutter doesn't manage the area well enough and allows the area to be cut to lower the water level which will happen if too much peat is taken from one area. That has an impact on the whole ecological landscape and is to be avoided. In some areas of crofting, dung was dried for the same purpose but I doubt the lovely taste and aroma of Whisky would be the same from dung smoke.

Looking from one longhouse to another.

Food

This would be a good point in our journey of discovery to touch on some of the food that the crofter would eat, though we have to remember that through certain times of history, the crofter had very little. He would eat what he had at hand but in times of plenty, the diet would be reasonable.

The crofter grew similar crops to those that had been available since the time of the Picts with newer and more robust varieties reaching them in the late part of the nineteenth century. Other than their main crops such as oats and barley, they grew leeks, onions, kale and legumes such as peas and beans. Once potatoes arrived in the later 1700s, it didn't take the crofter long to realise that a reasonable crop of potatoes could be grown from just the peelings. Generally, the crofter would be canny about what he grew and other than the crops he had to grow for the landlord, he would choose vegetables that gave the best yield for the ground.

Most crofts kept at least one cow and some had several, these being kept mainly for the milk. Milk products such as cheese and butter would be made at the croft and could be sold easily, which was preferable as it would not last long before going rancid, so it is likely that the family saw little of the milk from its own cattle.

Milk and cream separator.

There would also be hens for the eggs and also for the meat and a pig or sheep may also be seen on the crofter's land. During the many wars through the years that Britain has been drawn into, the crofter would make a reasonable profit from beef, for the British army would require much. But the Highland, 'black cattle' were scrawny beasts and not the favoured animal in the south. Nevertheless, when meat became short, everything would be purchased. Fish would be available closer to the coast and waste from the local fishing communities such as oil would be sought for lamps. Fish heads and tails were also acquired for dishes that we may frown upon today but in hard times would be a welcome boost to a boring diet. Dried fish would also be purchased as it would keep for longer though it could be of poor quality at times. There were also smokers at almost every major harbour and this would make a welcome change from dried fish.

Bere is an early type of barley.

The main crops were as stated previously oats and barley but the barley crop was a short-season type called bere. Bere is what is known as ninety-day barley which means it can easily be sown and harvested in the short season of the northern Highlands. It is nutritious and has more taste than modern barley and yet has the same uses including milling into flour for bread. Oddly, Rye has never been popular in Scotland and rarely occurs as a crop. This could be due to the fact that it grows tall and with the winds that usually claw their way across the Highlands, this means it would be ruined over the season. Even bere is sometimes grown within other crops to protect it and is still grown in Caithness and in Orkney. It has a particular taste and I should mention a story related to me by George Budge who at the time of writing lived in Orkney but was visiting the mainland for a short break. We were standing to the Northeast of the peaks of Scaraben and Morven and George mentioned that as a lad he had climbed Morven. Morven is the highest peak in Caithness and quite a strenuous trek even for a fit adult but George and his friends scaled it on a school trip. He related the story but he was adamant that the highlight of the trip was when they reached the base near Braemore. He takes up the story.

'There was a wee crofter's house at the roadside with a hazy plume of smoke from the chimney and I could smell peat smoke in the air. There was what I considered a woman of a certain age dressed in clothing from a previous era standing in the doorway of the house. She spoke with the teacher and we were offered scones, freshly baked by the lady. She explained that they were bere scones and I have to say, they were the best scones I have ever tasted. After

I was married, I told the wife about them and we have never had any other type of scone since.'

I can totally agree with George's account of these scones for like he, I consider bere scones a cut above the rest. Barbara Jane Gray had kindly given permission to reproduce her Beremeal and Sultana Scone recipe from her book, A Taste of Crofting. The full recipe can be found in the rear of the book.

I suppose this is the point I should quickly pass over the haggis. I am at risk of inviting the ire of fellow Scotsmen over my treatment of what is considered a traditional dish. There is no doubt that what is now called the haggis has some connection, not just to the crofter, but to all poor communities in the land. As I have already tried to show, the crofter would sell the best of his annual yield and make do with the parts that would not bring in so much profit. So, if an animal was slaughtered for food at any point, the better cuts would probably be sold off or used to barter for other things as the greater part could not be stored. The lights, or offal would not be wasted. As this would go off before anything else, it had to be processed and cooked as soon as it could. Therefore, it would be chopped up, mixed with oats and any other ingredients that were suitable and boiled in the stomach or hide of the animal. The haggis was a poor man's dish and if you look closely at the poem by Burns, I think it isn't celebrating the haggis, rather he's making fun of it. Before the poem, hardly anyone who had the means to eat better food would touch the stuff. The other irony is that it probably shouldn't be considered just Scottish.

There is a section in the verse cookbook *Liber Cure Cocorum* which was written in the 1430s in Lancashire, England.

For hagese'.
Þe hert of schepe, þe nere þou take,
Þo bowel noght þou shalle forsake,

On þe turbilen made, and boyled wele,
Hacke alle togeder with gode persole,

Translation:
The heart of sheep, the kidneys you take,
The bowel naught you shall forsake,
In the broth made, and boiled well,
Hack all together with good parsley,

There is also another reference from the same period describing a dish made from offal and herbs called 'hagws of a schepe'.

There is also an argument that it may have arrived with the Vikings too but I think it is likely it is much earlier and a version of it exists in most cultures.

There certainly are dishes that became truly Scottish, such as Cullen Skink and Cock-a-leakie soup, but these have been developed from earlier dishes. The main meal historically, would be the same as poorer communities around the rest of Britain and would be a pottage made with whatever was at hand along with porridge and other oat-based foods.

I ought to add a piece on a particular crofter's item I have seen on more than one occasion. But first, some background on salt. Yes, salt.

In the mediaeval period, salt was so regarded as a condiment and preservative that it could cost its weight in gold. Even through later centuries as it became easier to produce, it retained its throne on the better tables of wealthy people. It had its own place on the high table and was always flanked by two large spoons to denote its presence. Salt boxes and salt cellars would be highly decorative and sometimes made of precious metals with gems fixed to them.

The Roman soldiers were sometimes paid with salt for wages, it was so valued in their diet. This is probably where the word salary comes from. It was so important for preserving food too and allowed produce to travel much further making foods available to places where they had been rare.

By the time of the Industrial Revolution, methods for producing salt were improving but working in the salt industry was hazardous to health and it remained expensive compared to other foodstuffs. In the north of Scotland, the coming of the popularity of herring brought a massive need for salt to preserve the fish in the barrels and this had to be shipped in, as the East Coast of the Highlands has cliffs and few beaches. Places in England such as Saltfleet in Lincolnshire, had miles of flat beaches, ideal for a growing salt market. So-called 'salt roads', were built into the interior of England for salt caravans to take the produce to further markets. Ship-holds full of salt travelled from England and Europe to feed the demands of the herring industry in Scotland. Not until relatively modern times has salt become easy to produce and therefore become cheap. So, when I see early salt boxes that are from crofter's families I wondered how they afforded to fill such a large box. Eventually, I spoke to a lady from Aberdeen visiting Caithness to show her family where she was brought up and the kind of house she lived in. I showed her a large salt box and she admitted when she was a young girl, her family had such a box hung on the wall by the fireplace. I then asked her when money was scarce, how did they afford to fill such a salt box with salt.

'Och,' she smiled at me. 'We did'nae fill it with salt. My mather used tae put stanes in the bottom an' sprinkle a wee layer o' salt on the top so it looked like et wis full.'

This it seems was a pride issue to make it look like they were doing well for themselves. A case of keeping up with the Jones'. She also told me that when she was married and salt was cheaper, she had a large ceramic salt crock that sat on the hearth to keep the contents dry.

A Butt and Ben crofters house fallen to ruin. This unfortunately is how most of these dwellings look today.

The Land.

This is a wide subject but I am only going to skirt over it as there is little room to cover everything here.

It is impossible to generalise on this but though there are many areas of the Highlands where the soil is excellent, there are many where the soil is poor. There are also many areas where stones and rocks are more common than turf or soil. This meant that limited yields required more land to make a living. Ploughing this rocky ground was almost impossible until many of the stones were removed. If we then consider that before the age of the tractor, all that was available to the crofter was horsepower, you can see that it was time-consuming to prepare a piece of land for a crop. But horses have never been cheap to buy, and though the more successful crofter may have two animals, some had none and many ploughed with the use of a tool called a cas chrom. This tool is essentially a foot plough which means that ploughing the ground would have been hard, lengthy and laborious work.

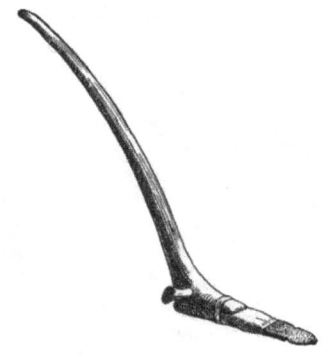

The cas chrom (bent foot) or foot plough.

In some references to Highland crofting, it is stated that the crofter had a heavy horse similar to a Clydesdale but this is not correct. Only larger farms run by wealthy landowners would have these expensive horses and the crofter would more likely use a horse known as a Garron or Garran. It is a tough little horse capable of heavy work and able to cope with slopes, yet is more economical than larger breeds and is still capable of working between the shafts of a cart. They are also smaller in height which enables them to easily be stabled in the low byre of a steading. This is the heavier of the small Highland pony which was bred on the mainland, the pony of Orkney usually being smaller.

I have spoken to at least two people from crofting families who have said that if there was just a single horse and it was ill or injured, then the woman of the house would be expected to take the harness for the plough. I am still unsure about this as I would suspect that even the strongest woman would struggle with the task and doubt even a burly man would have the strength to drag a plough through the rocky earth. The Garron, though bred for the work, is a very strong and capable horse.

A garron pony ploughing the rough ground.

The season in the north is short and this was an issue for the crofter as all the tasks from ploughing to harvesting were packed into this very short period. This left time out of season for other tasks but with very short days in the winter and very few means of lighting the croft during dark afternoons, once again these chores would have to be compressed into the short daylight hours. To say that this was a hard life is very much an understatement given the fact that the environment is unforgiving and harsh. Coupled with the fear of being moved on, your home being burned down, poor harvests and disease from the south, it is clear that the crofter was always fighting against long odds.

When anything modern or improvements were implemented, on most occasions there were celebrations. Over several years, I had the honour to get to know George Bethune, a Caithness man from generations of crofters. He poured many hours into research of his family and crofters in general as well as having a passion for local history. George is a well-read and well-travelled man now in his eighties but he has a fearsome memory and remembers his great uncle 'Beel' when he was still living in the Croft house at Lhaidhay. The house became a museum but George can tell a tale or two about his time there. He is also a very competent poet and the coming of mains water is recorded in his poem, Lhaidhay Remembered. Two verses in particular are of interest and are written in the old Caithness dialect.

No well across in Lappen,
Water wi' a cool clean taste.
Two pails ma load, as I crossed the road,
Wi' the gurd around ma waist.

And when the well was dry and dusty,
Then a trip for this young chap,
Doon til Toremore, where the water wid pour,
By chust turnan on a tap!

As can be seen, the water was still not piped to the croft and he still had to travel for it, if only a few yards further.
We will revisit George later in the book.

The lack of utilities and the small size of these mainly two-roomed dwellings ensured that eventually, most of them would be abandoned and forgotten. Plenty of them in various states of decay can still be seen in many places in the Highlands and Caithness seems to have more than anywhere else. Some are remote and so far away from roads that even in living memory, people recall having to travel miles to visit a shop. Malcolm Cameron told me a story about the travelling baker. Malcolm is now in his early eighties explained that he had to walk several miles along a track to the main road to visit a travelling baker. This baker would not traverse the rough track and would wait at the roadside. The young Malcolm would pick up the loaf wrapped in paper and trek all the way back to the homestead, pulling parts of the crust from the loaf and eating it as he made the return journey. He usually got a scolding or a 'clip round the ear' for stealing the bread.

I have a similar story of my own but I found a way to delay any chastisement. As a child, I did not have such a way to walk to the shop but I remember boring into the underside of the loaf as I walked home. It was some time before a slice being cut through the centre section of the loaf revealed a large hole where the bread had been removed for my snack.

In more modern times, Scottish bakers placed many loaves on the same tray and after baking they were separated and sliced. They are taller than other loaves and so produce a larger slice. A 'piece' is the usual way to describe a sandwich.

Thatching

Not all the crofter's dwellings were thatched. Some were covered in stone tiles and others had turf with nothing else covering it. Fortunately, we have a first-hand account of the tasks of keeping a thatch in good condition. We return to the accounts of George Bethune who in 2017, wrote down his memories of thatching in the 1940s and 1950s. This is a detailed account and so I will leave the reader in the capable hands of George. I have edited parts of this account as it covers other subject matter.

'In the late 1950s, my wife Nan and I attended an evening lecture in Edinburgh which included part of a paper on thatching. The lecturer asked if anyone could tell him why thatching in Caithness used straw, whilst in Sutherland they used reeds. I put my hand up and explained that in Caithness, straw was long and plentiful being a special variety. Also, it was not the first choice for winter feed. I went on to say that I had asked my relations in the Tongue area why they used reeds and not straw. They explained that in much of Sutherland, straw was used for feed and was too valuable to put on the roof. Both their hay and straw grew shorter than in Caithness and both were needed for winter feed. Reeds being abundant in their many lochs made it the obvious choice for thatching.'

'It is the case however that in the 1950s, the crofters turned away from growing oats and therefore the straw became scarcer and so even in Caithness, reeds became the choice for the thatch. We indeed used reeds cut from Loch Rangag.'

Author's note: What follows is George's explanation of some of the processes that went into the maintenance of the roof. The reader must understand that these stages need to be planned out as there are specific times of year for this to be done. For instance, the following passage covers the cutting of the turf which has to be done when the heather will regrow.

'To ensure a good supply of "divads", (divots) a relatively small area of heather-covered ground was burned so as to clear the rough heather. When the new growth was at a suitable height, using a lining spade and a flachter, we cut divads at about fifteen to eighteen inches broad and two feet long. The peat content was about two inches thick.'

Authors note: The thickness is to allow the roots of the heather to bind the substrate and prevent it from crumbling into pieces.

The Flachter or Flaughter.
These came with various-sized blades.

'These divads were then carted up to the house area then stacked and covered up. They were then ready for future use but is it worth noting that heather regrows quicker after being burned than it does when cut.'

'Then we come to the "bundles". When the sheaves are put through a Thrashing Mill, (sic) the individual stalks came out somewhat bent and twisted. In that state, they were built into the Corn Gilt.'

Author's note: The Gilt was the store of cut straw that was stacked neatly and covered or placed in a barn for the purpose.

'Sometimes, on a dry winter's morning, Great Uncle Beel and the young me would make "bundles". We would stand side-by-side in front of the straw gilt and pull out small handfuls of straw from the face of the gilt, running our fingers through it to straighten the straw. We would then set it by our feet on a straw band until the bundle was large enough and then the band was wrapped around it and tied with a knot. When we had made say a dozen each, we would take them to the barn for future use. We never thatched the roof all in one go. Only a nine or ten feet section was done at any one time.'

'A bright, sunny Saturday morning was always the first choice for re-thatching,' continues George.

'The net on the area to be worked was rolled back and ladders were put in position. The homemade metal holding hooks (made from fence wire) were pulled out and set aside for reuse. Then, the old straw thatch with its rat runs were thrown down and deposited in the muck-hole. An inspection of the straw-cleared roof was made to decide how many damaged divads needed to be replaced. The inspection

would be carried out by Great Uncle Beel and the thatcher, Donal O' Beels. (no relation)'
George continues.

'When Great Uncle Beel became too old, then I stepped in to take his place. Although weather and rat runs mainly damaged the straw thatch, some of the underlying divads could also need replacing, with divads always ensuring they were placed heather side down. Rat runs in thatch were unavoidable and common. At Lhaidhay they were from end to end despite cunningly laid traps.'

'The thatching, of course, started at the eaves, leaving a decent overhang and was expertly done in my time and for many years before that by Donal O' Beels. I passed the bundles up to Donal who took great pains to fit them nice and tight. Each bundle had its tying-straw band removed, flattened out a little and then pushed and prodded into place. It was then shaped by Donal using his hands and a wooden batten. He would then fix it in place with a reused or new metal hook.'

Author's note: Originally, these pegs or hooks would be a length of hazel twig, bent double and thrust into the heather turf below.

'Ever wary of the later inspecting eyes of David Lappen and Dod Bethune, Donal would make sure that the bottoms of each row of thatch were in perfect line by bashing any errant part even an inch or two. At the ridge, where the straw in an extra layer was bent over, I would sometimes stick in a harmless ornament just for fun. If the chimney was in the stretch being rethatched, then a good, thick 'scarf' of thatch was put around it which helped to stop the rainwater or melted snow from running down the inside.'

'When we had finished our work, the netting which was sometimes an old herring net, was pulled back on, re-tightened by rope along its bottom edge and weighted down with stones that had been collected from the shore. Lastly, the old seine net ropes were thrown over the roof five feet or so and also weighed down with heavy stones. Job done!'

Author's note: The winds that scour across this area of Caithness can be very severe and the strong Westerly's would blow the roof into the sea if it were not weighted down.

'We would step back,' continues George, 'admire our work and one of us would say, "not bad, not bad at all," and then we'd retire inside to visit Great Aunty Mary. Great Aunty Kirst (The Beeg Ammel) would be outside working.'

This incredible account by George must be quite unique and gives us a deep insight into the life of the crofter.

The very dwelling that George helped to thatch all those years ago. Here it is seen with a more modern and much shallower thatch than it would have had historically. It is now the Lhaidhay Croft Museum.

The People

There is, and has always been a world of difference between the Highlander and the Scot. The Highlander saw himself as different and a more independent person than the run-of-mill Scotsman. It is true that the two peoples have rarely got on throughout history but I am not about to try to explain that here, I will just state that they should be regarded as two different nations. Even the outsider that comes to live in the Highlands leaves his past at the border and encompasses the attributes that are still required to live in this harsh land and at times its inhospitable climate. So, there is little wonder that the people of the land are regarded a little suspiciously by those that do not understand the place.

The main differences between the Highland people and the rest of the United Kingdom usually revolve around the deeper sense of community and the need for mutual assistance in times of hardship. This can bring out characteristics that outsiders find odd such as their sense of humour. This humour can be very subtle at times and may be for the amusement of the perpetrator only. One story I heard from a Canadian chap probably illustrates this well enough. This Canadian gentleman was visiting Sutherland and Caithness on holiday and was trying to track down any living relatives with his own surname which was Clubb. He considered that there were no Clubbs left in the area and though I didn't know of any of that name, I doubted that all had gone. He explained that his ancestor moved to Canada during the clearances in the early 1800s and was lucky enough to find both good land and a reasonable landlord. He wrote to his relations still in the old country to tell them how well he was doing and gradually, most of them followed until all that the ancestor knew of were in Canada. Not being able to track down any Clubbs in Caithness or Sutherland he assumed that all, of that name had left or died out. I took his address and promised to pass his contact on to any Clubbs I may come across.

He also explained that the family connection with the old land remained and his grandfather would revert to Gaelic whenever he may have had a few too many to drink. When he was in his twenties, he asked his grandfather if he would teach him the old language so that he could speak the Gaelic. The grandfather raised his brows and told the young man he couldn't speak a word of Gaelic. When he pointed out that he would do so when several drams had passed his lips, he laughed and said it was just a ruse to make people think he could, it was just gibberish but no one realised it. He would even recite poems in his version of Gaelic. Luckily, he never came across a true Gaelic speaker.

A young crofting woman carrying peats.

Another example of the subtle humour of the land comes from George Bethune once again. His Great Uncle Beel had a very dry humour that to the casual observer could easily be missed but on one occasion during a severe winter, the village of Dunbeath on the coast of Caithness was many feet under the snow. George and his family lived in Dunbeath but Uncle Beel was still living on the croft up the hill. It was clear even from a distance that the snow had fallen so heavily and deep on the hillside that the croft house was almost buried. The snow had drifted and early one morning the family became worried for old Uncle Beel. George was eventually sent up the hill through the deep snow to make sure Beel was still alright. George being fairly tall soon found the snow was around his waist and in places he trod carefully as the road was impossible to follow. When he reached the Croft, the house was covered in snow from flagstones to thatch and all that could be seen of the building were the chimneys and the single window of the kitchen.

George panicked a little and forced his way through the snow to find the door and open it. He then smelled the unmistakable aroma of peat smoke and his panic subsided a little. He entered the kitchen to see Uncle Beel reading what must have been a two-week-old newspaper until he raised his head to view young George.

'Hello boy. Have y' come to see your Uncle Beel?'

'I came up to be sure you are well under all this snow.' replied George. Beel glanced towards the tiny window half-covered with snow and then back to George.

'So, are you telling me it's been snowing boy?' he asked.

It seems that the gentle and subtle humour of the crofter was a regular aspect of life and probably comes from the harshness of their history and the uncertainty of their existence. That isn't to say that this lifestyle was always so rigid. Children had their part in keeping the croft running from an early age but there were moments of relaxation and play.

For instance, Mary Gouch, a lovely lady who now lives in Frazerborough but spent her early life with her family on a croft, told me of her childhood. She told me much about the life of a young girl growing up in the harsh world of a crofting family but maintains they were some of the happiest times of her life. Her grandfather was born in 1866 and took on the croft just after the Crofter's Act of 1886. Though her father kept on the croft after *his* father died, she admits that the tales he told her were quite harrowing and the family had many hard times even after the Act came into being. Her father had told her of the failed crops and people having to beg back their produce to make ends meet. She told me that some people on land close to their croft left for Nova Scotia as late as the 1890s to try and escape poverty. Luckily for Mary, she only remembered good times from the early years she lived at the homestead. The croft was eventually let go when her father died, as her eldest brother took work as a farrier in Elgin and her younger brother went into the army. I saw a spark in her eyes as she told me how if she and her sister got up to mischief on the croft their punishment was always some task on the little farm. She told me about the task she hated the most.

'Me and my sister Juney had been down to the burn playing near a bridge and we suddenly felt hungry. We slipped back to the house where Mam had been baking. Whilst she went out to fetch some milk from the barn, we crept into the kitchen and thought it funny to steal two freshly baked scones from the rack on the kitchen table. We were unlucky as my elder brother saw us as he had been working at the hay barn. He told us to put them back.' She laughed at this point.
'We knew he would give us some task as punishment but Mam came back and asked what the fuss was and he told her what we had done. We expected to have to go and do some extra work as a punishment but she made us clean out the gulley in the Byre.'

Mary is referring to the trough that ran through the byre that took away all the mess that the cows made when in there.

'It was a horrible job but luckily it was summer and except for milking, the cows were kept outside. We decided not to steal any more scones or anything else for that matter.'

Mary had to do many tedious and onerous tasks but as she says, everyone in the family had a big part to play in ensuring all the work got done. She also remembered that she and her sister got into bother on wash day. It was their job to help with washing the family's clothes and on one windy day they didn't peg down the clothing well enough and had to find some items that had blown away. They then had to rewash them from scratch.

There were always such tasks to perform and of course, most of these were concerned with small farming chores such as growing crops. As mentioned previously, there were many crops grown but a long-term staple was the humble turnip. Turnip has been grown in Britain for thousands of years and had a more important role prior to the potato. For the crofter, it remained important, not just for the people but for winter feed for animals.

We return to George Bethune for a lesson in growing turnips. Neeps is the popular name for Turnips and swedes.

George explains, 'During my time in the 1940s and 50s, the growing of neeps was important and essential. They were usually planted and grown in a field that had recently grown corn. To prepare for planting the field would be disc harrowed then flat harrowed and finally grubbed with deeper pronged equipment that helped to break up the lumps.'

'With the field in good tilth, the two-sided plough formed the raise and pointed drills ready for seeding. Finally, the bought-in seed would be poured into the box designed for the task and carefully pulled along the top of each drill dropping seeds into the correct place.'

'Once the plants were two to three inches tall, they were thinned using a long-handled rake with a small metal end. Walking carefully along we would push or pull most of the young plants out leaving one every six inches or so. It was quite hard and skilful work but one I did from quite young.'

'Although there was a reasonable number of rows of turnips thinned at the croft, at the larger Knockglass Farm, the thinning of the neeps was a large task and was a well-organised Saturday job I looked forward to. A line of six or seven of us would start with much boasting and determination of being the quickest and best. No matter how hard myself and the others tried, we could never beat George Cunningham, (Pud) of Knockglass Farm.'

'When the neeps were fully grown,' continues George, 'and mature enough for harvesting, they were pulled from the ground and "docked". That is, the top and bottom cut off with a sharp blade with a wooden handle called a "docker". They were then loaded into a box cart and pulled by my favourite horse to the storage place. Although a few neeps were used to "knock the doors" or hollowed out with a carved face and a candle for Halloween, some were used by Great Aunty Mary for the table. For the most part, neeps were grown for feeding the animals, mainly the sheep. They were also used to swap for fish.'

Author's Note: The barter of produce was an essential part of the economy.

'Sometimes on a Saturday morning, I would spend an hour or so slicing neeps through our large cutter, hauling the big handle down as hard as I could, forcing the neep through the blades in the contraption. These cut pieces would then be scattered on the fields for the sheep to gobble down. The stronger sheep would shoulder the others "out of the nod" to get at them.'

'At that time, our breeding ewes were put to the sale at Latheronwheel, Wick or Thurso, usually when they were five years old. Their teeth at that age were worn down or missing. Years later, we found that feeding neeps to sheep rotted their teeth and that a diet excluding turnips resulted in North Country sheep producing lambs when they were eight or even nine years old.'

*A large turnip slicer.
These are sometimes incorrectly called a docker.*

The Famous – Hielan Coo

Mention should be made of one of the most distinctive animals kept by the crofter and during the 18th and 19th centuries, an important factor in the economy of the Highlands and Scotland in general. Crofters kept hens for eggs and meat and there would even be a pig on a few crofts but the most important Crofter's beast was the Highland Cow. They are very well known and their long shaggy coat makes them the obvious image for the tourist to Scotland but all that hair serves a purpose.

There are actually two versions of the Highland Cow. The larger, dun colour one with long hair and wide-set horns is the type that most people think of but there is another slightly smaller animal, usually black in colour but retains the hair and the horns. They were called Kyloe because of their ability to swim across the Kyles and lochs of the Highlands to reach the other side. I was even told of the herds that were gathered to swim across the Pentland Firth from Orkney to Caithness. I find this an incredible feat but several people have backed this up as being so. The Kyloe was mainstay of the Highland Croft and though not highly prised for meat in England, great herds were sent south to the midlands and the many markets there.

The 'black cattle of the Highlands', the Kyloe.

I should point out, however, that the word herd does not apply when it comes to the Highlander and his cattle as they were not herds but folds. This comes from the open but walled areas that the cattle were over-wintered in. Is this where the saying, 'back to the fold' comes from?

They are a hardy animal and they have two types of hair. The long, outer hair is water-proof and keeps the worst of the weather off the cattle, and then there is a softer, under-coat. This helps to keep the animal warm and insulates it from the harsh conditions. The hair covering their faces protects their eyes from the same conditions. They are also equipped with fearsome horns for defence against predators and though they have short legs, they can still turn a good pace for a short distance.

The breed was established in 1884 but no distinction was made between the two types. In 1954, Queen Elizabeth II ordered that Highland cattle would be kept at Balmoral where there are still representatives to this day. From small beginnings on the Western Isles, these cattle have become so popular that they were exported all over the world, particularly into countries where the weather is cold in the winters.

*John Stewart with 'Laoich' best of breed Perth show 1896.
This bull has had its long hair shorn.*

The Crofter at War

Though the absentee landlords were generally living in the major cities in the world, with little or no regard for the people they had forsaken, they would need them once again. This need did not come from a moralistic surge of national pride, it came from selfishness once more.

The Highlander has always been there to do his part. Not always by choice as the Battle of Culloden will testify. At Culloden, both sides had Highlanders who didn't wish to fight anyone, people who were threatened with beatings, burned houses or death. Brother faced brother on the field of Drummossie Moor, there at the beck and call of two commanders who had no interest in the Highlands or its people. Even so, the landowners scurried back to the Highlands when they needed troops to fight in the War of the First Coalition during the French Revolution.

Many battalions were raised, once again by threats or offers to the tenants to forget their arrears if their boys went to war. Further purges in recruitment followed in the further Wars of Coalition and into the Napoleonic Wars. Highland Regiments were a feature of just about every army at the time but they were considered troublesome after a series of mutinies.

I will not make comments about the naivety of the soldiers raised in this manner but it is clear that they were promised things at their recruitment that the King's Army could yet wouldn't comply with. That isn't to say that all the mutinies were for the same reason but nearly all were due to broken promises. To understand this, we have to look at the make-up of these battalions at a time when there were few permanent line regiments. The Highland Battalions took to wearing the short or small kilt as by the middle of the 18th century, it had become popular in the Highlands. The Philabeg (an Anglicised word from the Gaelic) was the name of this belted kilt and was even taken up by the British army for Highland units to distinguish these mainly Gaelic speakers from normal foot units.

Most of the dress of the Highlander was very different to other British soldiers and they looked so exotic to English eyes that the public turned out by the thousands to watch them march south. They were led by a piper and drums which made them even more other-worldly and they must have caused a stir wherever they were deployed. This meant that the Highlander didn't want to transfer into other units as it would mean their unique dress would be lost, causing a determined attachment to the battalions they were recruited to. This simple conditioning had been an issue on at least one of the mutinies.

Highland Trooper around 1800

Another reason was a promise to certain regiments, one being the 43rd Foot, the Black Watch, (later the 42nd Foot) being sent to England whilst the English line infantry were sent abroad. The Watch were told that they, nor the other Highland troops would be sent abroad. When they found this to be a lie, a mutiny ensued and the Highland Regiments set off home.

Many of these mutinies failed to resolve the issues and after ringleaders were shot or hung, the troops ended up going to where they were told, sometimes never to return. Disease caused many more fatalities in foreign service than any amount of campaigning. This was the reason that most did not wish to go abroad but there was also another not unreasonable issue.

Most of the regiments were not paid. This was true of the English troops too because then as now, Government departments were corrupt, inept or both and in those days it was certainly both. The 76th Foot were paid £2000 in arrears before they would leave the shores of Edinburgh. At the end of the war, the 77th Foot mutinied for several reasons including a change of equipment and pay, but their biggest complaint was that the war was over and they were being sent to India where the life expectancy was short through disease. They pointed out that when they were recruited they were promised that they were signed up for three years or until the war ended. The war was at an end and they had done their bit and wished to return home. They occupied the barracks in Edinburgh and refused to go to the ships. Their plight reached parliament and strangely they did receive some support. It is worth noting that even these mutineers were always considered to be well behaved and with the exception of a few isolated drunk troopers, they conducted themselves admirably. It was said that they would still come to the parade ground even without their officers, clean, tidy and shaven and with the highest level of restraint and discipline.

Eventually, after several posters and bills reached parliament, some of which the Highlanders had carried on their persons throughout their service, the truth of the veracity of their claims was proven and they won their cause. They were sent north back to the Highlands and their deserved discharge.

As stated, there were many reasons for the mutinies but the one that seems to have caused the most ire to the Highlanders and the public of Scotland for that matter, was the raising of the regiments by these absentee landlords who lived in England.

Seaforth Highlanders

When parliament needed to raise armies, some of the wealthier landowners and clansmen living in England decided to travel to their lands and raise a battalion or two for the war effort. Not through any deep-rooted concern for the British Empire or to help defend the shores of Britain, but to win commissions in the army. Being a Lieutenant Colonel or even a major would do their business interest no harm and would help also in their social circles. Some of them struggled to raise men, however, and those that did, usually abandoned them before they went abroad and were handed over to an English commander or worse, a lowlander. Battalions being sent to the Americas during the American War felt they were being sold out and one battalion heard from the public that they would be sent to India and sold as mercenaries to the East India Company. It wasn't entirely true, but the Highlander had a deep-rooted sense of honour that no one except a Highlander would understand. Incidents like this didn't help the cause of Clan Chiefs and wealthy men of substance in the eyes of the Highland soldier. It seemed to them they were being abandoned yet again.

By the time of the Great War and the Second World War, the political and social climate had changed and Highlanders volunteered in their thousands to join the British Army to defend the Commonwealth. Unfortunately, by this time, their regard was considered so high by the British Establishment that Highland and Scottish Regiments were used in just about every major theatre during these two wars. Further reading about the history of the Highland Division (sometimes called the Highway Decorators) will attest to this.

*Soldiers of the 72nd Highlanders
Photograph by Joseph Cundall and Robert Howlett.*

However, overuse of these regiments led to a massive disparity in the casualties compared with the Welsh and English, which has caused some commentators to describe them as 'cannon fodder'. I'm not sure I totally agree with this but I think that the reputation of the Highlander in wars is so high, that the legend outstrips the truth and sometimes they were expected to work miracles. To a certain degree, it was a Scotsman who was responsible for this state of affairs, not an Englishman. Henry Dundas, the Home Secretary, later, eventually elevated to the Secretary of War, who in 1793 decided to reform parts of the army. He was the head of an inefficient, chaotic and corrupt organisation whose ideas outpaced his abilities. At the time, the population of Scotland was one-fifth of that of England and Wales. Only three per cent of the king's subjects lived in the Highlands yet over the next seven years many new 'fencible' foot regiments and horse regiments would be raised. Sixty, foot regiments and forty-six horse regiments would be raised and yet Scotland would supply thirty-seven foot regiments and thirteen horse regiments. And twenty-three of these were Highland troops. Thirty-eight per cent of the King's foot soldiers were Highlanders and this disparity would remain throughout the history of the British army. To a degree, the need for Highlanders in the army was the only thing that slowed down the clearances as Lord Selkirk wrote in 1805.

'Gentlemen who still had the means of raising their tenants, suspended for a time the extension of sheep farming and the progress of the advance of rents.' All this meant that when the few men who returned from the war went back to their shires, they found their blackened homesteads with no roofs, their families scattered and sheep grazing where once was a township. A fitting thanks indeed for fighting for their king. It certainly turned the tide in respect of men joining the British army.

Archibald Stewart sang,
'If I were as I used to be,
Amongst the hills,
I would not mount guard,
As long as I lived,
Nor would I stand on parade,
Nor for the rest of my life,
Would I never put on a red coat.'

Soldiers were raised where they could be and some were dressed like jongleurs and jugglers in hideous theatrical representations of their traditional dress to their embarrassment. But once they were sent on their way to war, pay was held back and clothing and equipment were in short supply. In this climate of utter stupidity, tens of millions of pounds were squandered by piratical self-serving people like Colonel Delancy, given the post of Barrack Master by William Pitt the younger. When it was realised that he squandered over nine million pounds, he was asked to retire lest his incompetency and corruption brought down the government. He did so and even after this disgraceful show of disregard for morality, he was still given £6 a day pension for the rest of his life which amounted to two hundred times the wages of the foot soldier. In light of more recent scandals with the leadership of

Scotland, it seems the people have been brutalised by their own countrymen throughout history.

It is ironic that the Scottish Soldier has remained loyal to the Union throughout this period and none more so than the Highlander.

Either way, the many white crosses in Flanders or the many war memorials carry hundreds of thousands of names of men who went away to defend Britain but never came home to enjoy peace.

Black Tam

Julia Wilson sent me this story for which I am most grateful and she says it was a well-worn tale when she was a child. She first heard the story in the late 1940s and it was told to her by her mother. It concerns a man by the name of Thomas Hoy who seems to have been quite a character. He went for a soldier at the age of just fifteen in 1808 and spent his early career as a drummer. The following year he was transferred to the 92nd (Gordon) Highlanders. (I cannot find Thomas's name or the original Regiment he was in but my research into the history of the 92nd has revealed much information that gives veracity to the tale. I have included what I have learned and filled in the gaps of the tale with it.)

Due to the regiment being involved in the disastrous Walcheren Campaign, the newer recruits were held back in England to await the return of the Regiment. The unit returned with less than half its men, many lost in the retreat and the others too sick to remain in combat. Under these dark days, the young Thomas joined his fellows. By then it had been renamed the 92nd Regiment of Foot and when reinforced and resupplied they returned to Portugal under General Viscount Wellesley in September. It is likely that Thomas saw much action as the regiment partook in many major battles from 1811 through until 1813 as the 92nd are known to have been heavily involved in this campaign. The regiment then pursued the French Army into France and further battles followed including the Battle of Toulouse. We cannot know what part Thomas took in the battles if any but the unit certainly took an active part. When they returned to England, Thomas was reputed to be a Corporal at the age of twenty so we have to assume he was a reasonable soldier. In 1815 the regiment returned to the continent for the Hundred Days Campaign and was at both Quatre Bras and Waterloo. This in itself is an impressive achievement and from what we know of the level of fighting at these two engagements, Thomas Hoy was no stranger to action. We know from the records of the Regiment that they repulsed a bayonet charge from the French at Quatre Bras.

Three days later at an early stage in the epic Battle of Waterloo, Napoleon's troops attacked the left of the Allied line, and the 92nd was ordered to charge the leading French column. They did as ordered and the French column broke in disorder. When the Scots

Greys passed through the regiment to get to the scattering French troops and press the advantage, some members of the regiment clung to the stirrups of the passing Greys so that they could get at the French. Corporal Dickson of "F" Troop of the Scots Greys, reported:

'They were all Gordons, and as we passed through them they shouted "Go at them the Greys! Scotland for ever!" My blood thrilled at this and I clutched my sabre tighter. Many of them grasped our stirrups and in the fiercest excitement, dashed with us into the fight.' We have no way of knowing if Thomas was involved but it illustrates the environment he was in. The regiment returned to Edinburgh on the 7th of September, 1816 and was cheered by a large crowd. Many of the men in the regiment were from Aberdeenshire but Thomas was a Sutherland man.

He had left the army by 1817 and returned to Sutherland but his brother took ill and Thomas moved to the croft to help him. From this point on, I cannot verify any of the story that Julia sent me, but as some snippets of information she related tie in with what I have found, I have no reason to believe that any attempt to sensationalise the story has been made by her family over the years that the story has been told.

It seems that not long after his return from war, he was involved in a small riot when the factors came to force several families from their homes. Constables were brought in and many people were hurt. Thomas had to flee the area to prevent being restrained and eventually settled near Burghead. He developed a fearsome reputation and it was said he had killed twenty Frenchmen at Quatre Bras alone. He became known as 'Black Tam' and even at the age of sixty-eight, it was said he could knock a man out with a single punch. He never married and ended his years with his younger sister whose husband died at an early age. It is thought that Thomas died around 1883 at ninety years of age. This certainly fits with his history and timeline.

Julia's grandfather William, when he was just a lad, knew Black Tam as the quiet but dark character who would sit by his door with a pipe when the sun shone. William told many stories about Black Tam when he himself was in his old age, the favourite being about 'Young Jack'.

As Thomas never married and his sister was in her sixties when she shared the little house with her brother, Julia's grandfather, William, was just a young lad but was surprised to see a crib just inside the door of the house. The young William was one of the few people that Thomas would speak with, mainly because William would do chores in exchange for eggs or some other small gift. When he asked why Black Tam had a crib, Tam looked back at the crib and then back to the young lad.

'It's for Young Jack'. The lad asked who Jack was, as the man was already very old and unmarried.

'He's new-born jus' this month,' replied Tam in his gruff voice. William was now very curious that there was a bairn in their family.

'Can I see?' he asked cautiously as Tam was known to have a temper. Tam just shrugged and stared out at the world in general saying,

'Aye, but dunna wake him if y' dunna want a skelpin'.' William tentatively and carefully squeezed past the seated Tam and stepped into the dark interior. The crib was well made and had good clean linen fitted. William slowly pulled back the linen and he was shocked by what he saw. There was a tiny wee kitten fast asleep. William petted the kitten and it made a contented stretch but William quickly replaced the covers remembering Tam's warning about not waking Young Jack.

'Did you see him?' asked Tam momentarily removing the pipe from his mouth. William nodded and allowed a slight smile.

'Can I come and see him again?' William asked. Tam frowned and once again removed the pipe.

'Aye,' he growled, 'but if y' mention it to another soul, I'll drown you an' Jack in the same water butt.'

I love this story as it really shows how a person corrupted by so much death and violence can still show affection for things beyond the horrors of men.

The Big Ston

We now return to George Bethune. This is a story told to me some time ago by him but it is one that I do not have notes for, so it is from memory.

George's Great Uncle Beel had done all the jobs he had to complete for the day and leaned on a fencepost contemplating the land and considering what needed to be done the following morning. He then noticed the 'big ston'. A large flat rock that had stood outside the byre since anyone could remember. No one knew why it was there or even if it had been there since time began. It was such an anomaly, that there was no choice other than to attach stories to it or a legend. This is what happened. A legend grew locally around the rock and why it was there. This legend metamorphosed into a treasure legend as many such stories do. It was never clear how the treasure got there but everyone became convinced that under the great stone lay a king's ransom in treasure. Many times, Beel had glanced over at the stone and it is more than possible that he saw the story as 'an old wives tale' but this day as many others his eyes had rested on the stone and he wondered what was actually under it. Also, like many other days, he quickly forgot about it and got on with his work.

Later in the day, his brother Dod came by and the two got to talking about the weather and the season when Dod's eye was also caught by the 'big ston'. Beel noticed his gaze but ignored it and gave a little chuckle to himself.

'You know,' began Dod still looking at the stone, 'one day we should move that ston' and see what's under it.' Beel stopped and looked up from his task and followed Dod's gaze.

'Aye,' replied Beel, 'but you can'nae undo what you know.' Dod looked at Beel with a puzzled look.

'What do you mean?' asked his brother.

'As we stand here,' explained Beel, 'that big ston' has purpose. It has treasure under it and many wid say the same.' This was obvious to Dod and his brow furrowed still not sure what Beel was getting at. 'But if we move it and find nothing under, it's just a big ston'.'

'I see what y' mean,' nodded Dod. 'But it wid be nice to know one way or the other.' The two men agreed it would but how would they move it? They doubted that even two horses would be able to shift it due to its weight and it would have to be freed from the embrace of the earth to even stand a chance of being dragged. The only option was to dig under it. They chose a day and vowed that they would make a serious attempt to find what was under the stone. On the chosen day, Dod arrived and had brought his good spade ready for the hard work at hand. When Beel appeared, he was not carrying his own spade and Dod wondered if he had changed his mind.

'Are you not ready to give it a go?' asked Dod.

Aye,' nodded Beel giving the stone a hard stare.

'So will you fetch your spade so we can work from both sides?' asked Dod. Beel glanced at Dod and said,

'I'm thinking, if we used some intelligence, we could make this easier.'

'I'd rather use my spade,' smiled Dod holding up the instrument. Beel walked to the stone placing his hand upon it and then speaking.

'There is a way til break the stone into two pieces.'

'Fire and water you mean?' frowned Dod. 'It's a big ston til break so.' Beel nodded at this but was sure it could be done. So, they set about breaking the stone just as the ancients had done. They gathered what timber they could find and dug out a small hole under the stone. They piled up kindling on the top of the stone and a little under it in the hole. The kindling was set alight and timbers were placed on the fire until a good blaze was going. Then they stood back and watched the fire. As they watched, the stone turned dark where the fire was blazing and as the fire died, they swept away the embers and trickled cold water over the stone. There was steam but not much else.

'It's not hot enough,' insisted Beel and they looked around for anything else they could burn. Few trees grew in Caithness and wood was always difficult to find and usually too precious to burn. It was better to use it for repairs but they scouted around and brought all they could find to the stone. Once again, a fire was started before the stone could fully cool and this time they used every bit of combustible material they could find and set a very hot fire going below and above the stone. This time when they had brushed away the dying embers, they could feel the stone was much hotter than previous and the water poured on created more steam than the morning fish train from Helmsdale. Then, there was a dull sound. Not a crack but more like a thump and they looked down to see that the stone was at last split. Their idea had worked but now the two halves were still of a great size and would need spade work and the horse to part them. Bars were used to pry the halves apart and ropes tied around one of them. The earth at the base of the stone was dug away and the horse hitched to the rope. The little garron pony knew his work well and leaned into the harness to pull the weight behind him the best he could. With help from Dod and Beel, the stone began to move. Once there was enough of a gap between the stones, Dod reached for his spade and they took turns to dig. Of course, no treasure was found and as Beel had suggested, they had found nothing and lost something. They had lost the legend of the 'big ston'. What they had achieved however, was proving that an ancient way of breaking stones could be done and the satisfaction of overcoming obstacles and solving a problem was good enough. Over the years, the two stones were moved and no one can remember where the two pieces went. They were probably used for shoring up some loose ground or redirecting a stream.

Many years later when water mains were first laid at the side of the main road, the contractors were digging a trench for the pipes and came across two massive stone blocks. They were not like the 'big ston' but they were large enough for the contractors to bring in equipment to remove them. When the pipes were laid and covered over, the stones lay where they were dropped for many years. One was moved for some purpose or other but the remaining one still sits where it was left to this day. Could it be that one day in a thousand years some person will start a legend of treasure under that stone, and maybe someone will break it in two with fire and water? Probably not.

'Bliadhna nan caorach' - The Year of the Sheep

To conclude our story, we will slip back into the past to explain a little more why the Highlander and Lowlander had (and still have in some areas) a mutual distaste for each other.

The army regiment known as The Black Watch is seen by many Scots people as a proud legacy of the toughness and fighting spirit of the Scottish people. Yet to a greater degree, this is due to later propaganda and a lack of knowledge of the regiment's prior history previous to the two world wars.

The 42nd Foot as they were known (prior to this being the 43rd) were one of several 'watches' formed as a way to curb the rebellious nature of the Highlander. To the Highland population, these watches were a military force meant to keep order and bring felons to justice and so they quickly became disliked and described as *Am Freiceadan Dubh,* the black or dark watch. Far from being the hero of many a battle, they were hated and despised as puppets of the British parliament with their own agenda through their commanding officers.

They were used in this role for many years and in 1792, they would see action again to quell the Highlander.

The innocuous Cheviot Sheep

On July 27th, crofters in the Strathrusdale area hatched a plan to collect all the sheep in the area and drive them south. The plan was announced at several churches around Sutherland and Easter Ross on the following Sunday, and by Tuesday 200 or more crofters were droving thousands of lowland sheep toward Inverness to protest about the incursion of the animals. Local landlords quivering in their expensive riding boots sent frantic correspondence to Edinburgh and London. Henry Dundas ordered three companies of the 42nd, (Black Watch) then stationed in Inverness, to disperse the protestors. No shots were fired but the protest fell apart. The ringleaders were arrested and taken to Inverness Prison. They were tried in September: and two were sentenced to transportation but managed to escape, probably with help.

The reasons for the fear in the landowner's minds need far more examination than we have room for here, but we have to remember that most of the clan chiefs had already sold out their people for money and with riots in Birmingham and the revolution in France, England and lowland Scotland saw the Highlanders as a violent mob stirred up by general resentments *'against property and social order'*. At the same time, journalists from the Edinburgh Courant and Caledonian Mercury saw it as a *'Revolutionary response to the poverty and oppression brought by rapacious landlords'*. Little wonder that the wealthy saw their way of life under threat. If it could happen in

France, it could possibly happen at home. Of course, 200 crofters were no threat. They just wanted their way of life back.

Still, Sir George Mackenzie of Aberdeenshire, who documented the 1792 protest in his 1810 General View of Ross and Cromarty referred to the protestors as a "mob" and to the Highlanders as "natives". This shows prejudices akin to the colonial settlers across the Atlantic towards the indigenous tribes of North America.

Whatever we feel about the clearances and whichever stance we take, there is no doubt that the Year of the Sheep represents an Indigenous Highland stand, against what we now call 'slow violence'. That is, a gradual and largely unseen but hugely damaging effect, that modern capitalists have wrought on nature and peoples throughout the world. In short, the exploitation of the land comes before the people of the land and the *White Wave* which was the Cheviot sheep was always about a few people making vast profits rather than the whole population making a living.

The irony is that the clearances still go on. The sheep is now a staple of the local farmer and crofter alike and the fertile fields that saddle the A9 seem to be blanketed with Cheviot and black-faced sheep. What began as a scourge has become a profitable living for many farmers.

But no longer does the sway of the Duke and Duchess of Sutherland oppress the land and the people, but the clearances continue though it is not the sheep who are to blame this time.

The new overlords are the electricity-generating companies that constantly pressure land-owners to sell land to allow the generating infrastructure to exist. The White Wave is now regiments and armies of wind turbines and pylons taking electricity to England and the lowlands. It has become impossible to look out to sea and not see turbines watching over the land. The far north is still difficult to survive in. Everything costs more and nothing can be taken for granted. People move to the north for the natural beauty, the clean air and to be closer to nature. Where was natural beauty and wilderness, now sits the lust for profit and ugly machinery. The environmentalist's purge to build renewable energy sources is having a devastating effect on the area actually causing a carbon footprint that the Far North isn't used to. This is caused by the heavy machinery needed to build and maintain this equipment and so once again the population's is beginning to decline. Even the Highland Council have admitted that numbers are declining in Caithness and Sutherland. There are many outsiders who have moved to the north to make this their home and they are passionate about the area, but as in the time of the crofters, their few voices cannot be heard above the clamour for profit.

There are many reasons for population decline, not just the reason I have alluded to above but for now, the Highlands has to content itself that it has entered yet another era of its history, and hopefully, it and its people will survive and thrive still.

Appendix

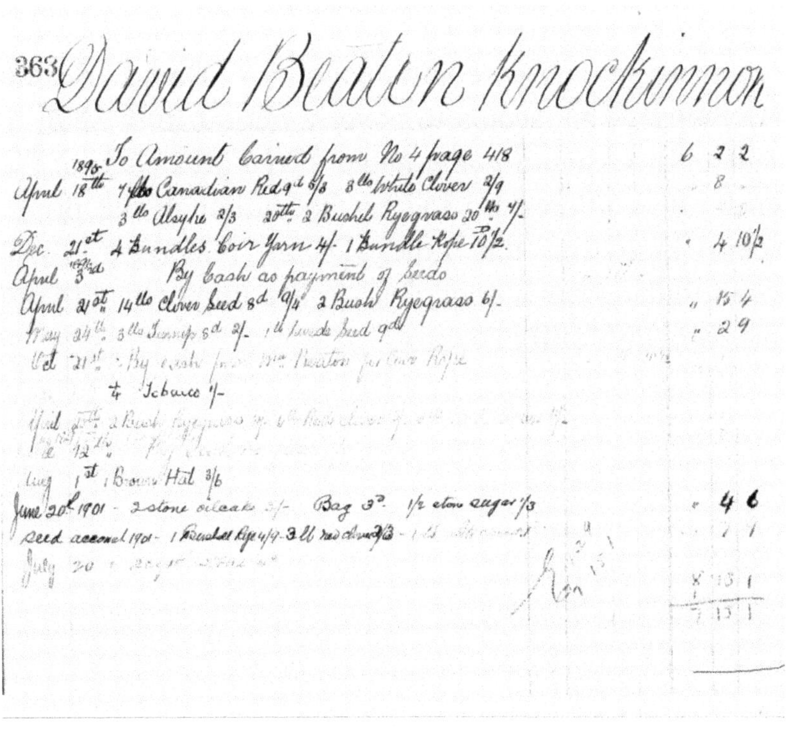

[Handwritten ledger page, transcription approximate:]

363 David Beaton Knockinnon

1895 To Amount Carried from No 4 page 418   6 2 2
April 18th 7 ℔ Canadian Red 9d 5/3 8 ℔ White Clover 2/9   8
           3 ℔ Alsyke 2/3 20th 2 Bushel Ryegrass 20 ℔ 7/
Dec. 21st 4 Bundles Coir Yarn 4/- 1 Bundle Rope 10/2   4 10½
April 3rd   By Cash as payment of Seed
April 21st 14 ℔ Clover Seed 8d 9/4 2 Bush Ryegrass 6/-   " 15 4
May 24th 3 ℔ Turnips 8d 2/- 1 Bundle Seed 9d   " 2 9
Oct 21st - By cash from Mrs Beaton for Coir Rope
          ¼ Tobacco 1/-

April 5th 2 Bush Ryegrass 9/- ...
   " 12th   ...
Aug 1st 1 Brown Hat 3/6
June 20th 1901 - 2 stone oilcake 3/- Bag 3d ½ stone sugar 1/3   " 4 6
Seed account 1901 - 1 Bushel Rye 4/9 - 3 ℔ red clover 3/3   " 1
July 20 ...
                                                           8 13 1
                                                           7 13 1

Opposite is an account page for David Beaton (Bethune). That seems to cover a period from 1896 to 1901. Knockinnon is the name of the area close to the croft. It is interesting to see that although the prices seem high for the time, David (George's Great Grandfather) has a good years grace to pay his bill but was probably still in arears.

George Bethune's poem in its entirety.

LHAIDHAY REMEMBERED

Lhaidhay looked small, courried.
As I passed the other morn.
Windows dark, no peat fire spark,
A hoose diminished, forlorn.

No Curst, no Beel or Mary,
Sittan roond the fire,
No milkan coo, or fatnan soo,
And an empty stable and byre.

No Pixie til bark a welcome,
Or give ye a growl or two,
No slinkan cats, after mice an' rats,
In the thatch, or the corn stack screw.

No scratchan hens or chickens,
Or pampered cheviot flock,
No ducks or geese, efter a piece,
Then chasean the Rhode Island cock.

No fields o' bere or wavean corn,
Cabbage, tatties or neeps.
In horse ploughed fields, by Dondle O' Beels,
There's a tractor driven by Peeps.

Fields in aged rotation,
Cultivated wi' graip spread dung,
Workan scythe or sheet, lamban a sheep.
Tasks to leard whilst young.

No lines for Monday's usual wash,
Or peatstack built bonnie by Beel.
No waitan for news, when the cornyard screws,
Would be threshen by Allan's Mill.

No sight or sound o' Mary's churn,
Makean butter so loved by Mam.
And once a year 'Beastie' was exceptional tasty,
Lek the cruddy and homemade jam.

No well across in Lappen,
Water wi' a cool clean taste.
Two pails ma load, as I crossed the road,
Wi' the gurd around ma waist.

And when the well was dry and dusty,
Then a trip for this young chap,
Doon til Toremore, where the water wid pour,
By chust turnan on a tap.

No roadside sign for 'Rowats Tea',
Til catch each passan eye.
And studs at night, showed the message bright,
As vehicles drove by.

No big ston cracked by Dod and Beel,
Left lyan ootside the byre,
Not broke for pleasure, but lookan for treasure,
And split by water and fire.

The Box and Long Cairts vanished,
My horse pulled trips no more,
For peats til the hill, corn til the mill,
Or sometimes doon til the shore.

And as I passed the other morn,
Ma thoughts went back to us thatchan.
Wi, 'bundles' o' straw, through fingers we'd draw,
Then fix them all neat and matchan.

And as we thatched, auld Beel wid tell,
How the Bethunes were cleared from Rockhead.
That in 1835, nine took the short drive,
Til build and thatch this homestead.

Great uncle Beel wis the last til live,
In the croft house called Lhaidhay.
Slim and small, he wis loved by all,
For his charm and his gentle way.

Lhaidhay is now a croft museum,
Where visitors examine and learn,
Of hard work and strife, but a healthier life,
On the Bethunes' old small farm.

Taken with permission from Barbara Janes Gray's book A Taste of Crofting.

Barbara's Beremeal and Sultana Scones

Ingredients
8oz Self Raising Flour
2 oz Beremeal
2 oz Caster Sugar
2oz Butter.
2oz Sultanas
1/2 tsp Baking Powder
Pinch Salt
Milk
Water to mix.

(Alternatively use plant milk and lemonade / tonic. I use lemonade as it acts well as a raising agent and makes the scones a little lighter and sweeter than milk.)

Method
Sift the flour, beremeal, baking powder and salt into a bowl. Rub the butter into the dry ingredients until it forms a breadcrumb like consistency. Add the sugar and sultanas and mix well.
Add the liquid until you have a light but not sticky, soft dough. Do not over handle as this will prevent the

dough from rising well. If you have time, the dough should be covered with cling wrap and put in the refrigerator for 1-2 hours.
Gently roll out to approximately 2" thick and cut into circles with a pastry cutter or glass. Should make 10 – 12 scones depending on the size of your cutter.
Place on a lightly greased baking tray and bake in a preheated oven 425 F / 200 degrees C / Gas7 for 15 – 20 minutes until brown.

The author is greatly indebted to many people who have spent their valuable time to relate the stories included in this book.
In particular, George Bethune who was the inspiration for the work. Also, George Budge, Malcolm Cameron, Julie Wilson, Mary Gouch and Alan Rosey.

If you have enjoyed this book, please consider the further books in the Highland Histories series.

A Taste of Crofting - Barbara Jane Gray
A Tale of Crofting – Alex McGlashen
A Matter of Survival – Alex McGlashen – out 2025

These and other books available from
Trick Imp Publishing
www.trickyimp.com